CHARLES AND DIANA'S TOUR OF NORTH AMERICA

PHOTOGRAPHY
DAVID LEVENSON
TEXT
TREVOR HALL

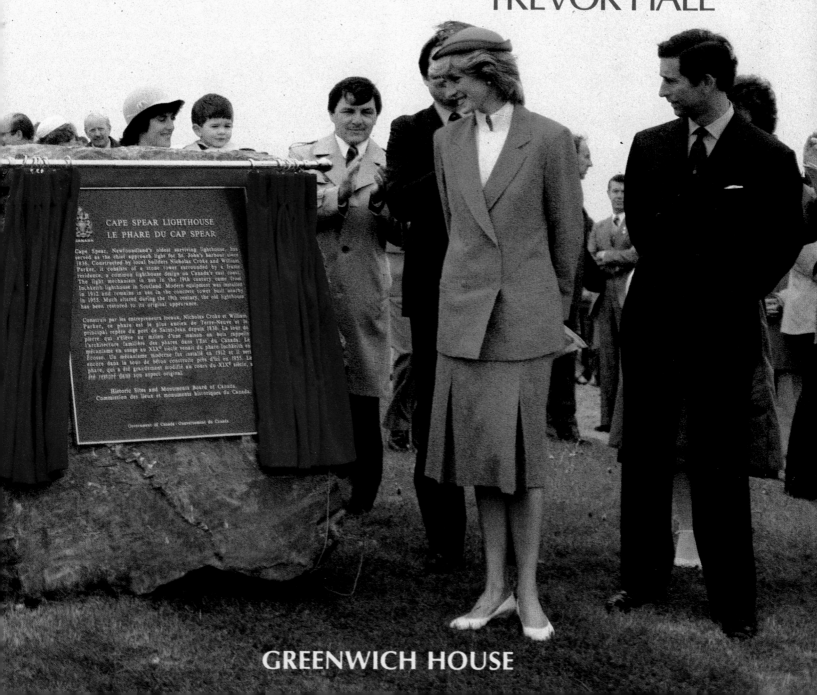

GREENWICH HOUSE

Flags had been waving frantically from the moment the Prince and Princess of Wales' aircraft was spotted circling Shearwater Air Force Base at Halifax. The almost hysterical surge of cheering on their arrival set the tone for their first walkabout at the Garrison Grounds, to a spontaneous, exhuberant, Nova Scotian welcome.

This historic day – 14th June –
called forth great national pride,
and the flags proclaimed it
powerfully. But the Princess
made her own contribution by
wearing a striking outfit in the
colours of the maple-leaf flag.
Fair skies and a gentle breeze
gave the occasion a carnival
atmosphere and everyone, it
seemed, was shouting, "We want
Di!"

Weatherwise the welcome didn't last. Wednesday 15th June dawned dull and rainy as the Prince and Princess visited HM Canadian Dockyard to inspect a new naval repair depot. Amid the scaffolding of the unfinished building —to be named after the Prince upon completion— they unveiled the first of scores of commemorative plaques awaiting them on their fortnight's tour. After a musically memorable visit to St George's Church to launch its restoration scheme they made for Halifax Commons for their second walkabout in less than 24 hours.

Mercifully the rain abated: to the crowds' delight there were no umbrellas, no raincoats. Prince Charles looked natty in a double-breasted suit, while the Princess' beige-trimmed, off-white coat-dress and matching pill-box hat, veil and bow, provided a bright focal point on a dull day. Indeed there was plenty of colour about. A newspaper photographer sported a fabric pigeon, and thousands of schoolchildren released a sky-ful of balloons as a spectacular finale to their patriotic songs. However, one Union Jack was comparatively faded. Dating from Queen Victoria's Diamond Jubilee, it was shown by its proud owner to the Princess. "It's nearly as old as him," she remarked, eyeing Prince Charles!

Meeting the people involved
listening to them, and to their
music. A massed band of a
thousand ukuleles strummed
popular favourites and three
thousand soaked and shivering
schoolchildren, accompanied by
a pianist whose hands played
uncertainly upon keys hidden
beneath protective tarpaulins,
serenaded their visitors. "Will Ye
No' Come Back Again?" they
sang, —and it was difficult to
deny that the idea sounded a
good one.

The royal spurning of raincoats until the last minute was no mere bravado. Despite the appalling weather, the walkabout and tree-planting ceremony were totally unhurried. Both visitors devoted time as much to rewarding people for loyal patience as merely to meeting them. It was New Zealand all over again: popular then for not diving for shelter even in the worst weather, the royal couple worked the miracle again in Halifax.

Persistent yells of "We want Di"
brought forth the miracle again
that evening. Arriving wrapped
in a black cape, she looked
entrancing. When, once inside,
she removed it to reveal a
magnificent cream silk gown, the
guests seemed to applaud for
ever.

The menu for this first official banquet was aristocratic without being extravagant – pâté de fois, poached sole with vegetables and salad, apple meringues, Canadian wines. Premier Trudeau chatted happily with the Princess – a picture of poise and regality, her jewellery glittering behind the banks of table-flowers. Indeed he seemed charmed by her, urging Prince Charles to take a Government job "as chief guide to Her Highness. You would not find the pay very high, but the company would be very pleasant." Informal, witty speeches included the Prince's despairing comments on Nova Scotia's weather. The visit of the future King Edward VII in 1860 was marred by rain. "Nothing changes," sighed Prince Charles.

The Loyalists were out in force
and traditional costume, to
welcome the royal couple to
Shelburne on 16th June; proudly,
for this was their first ever royal
visit. The traditional fishing boat
– the dory – is still built here, so
much was made of their tour of
the Shelburne Dory Shop – now
commemorated by a plaque.

From Shelburne they drove – the fog was too heavy for a helicopter flight – to Bridgewater, where a lobster buffet-luncheon awaited them. The Prince was duly bibbed, but his wife refused, fearing for her flamenco-style hat. Prince Charles brought the community "the belated gratitude of the late King George III for your unswerving loyalty and devotion to the British Crown."

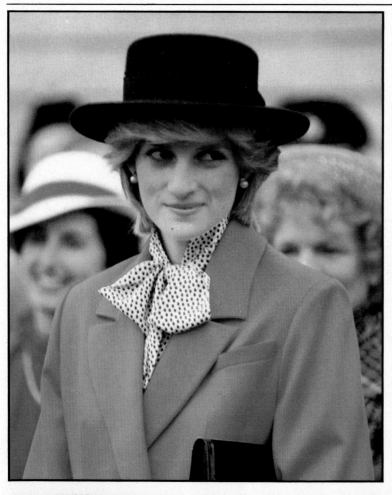

Britannia sailed into Saint John to begin the royal visit to New Brunswick on 17th June. Prince Charles called it "St John's", but the excited screams of welcoming schoolchildren made it clear that a walkabout easily prompts forgiveness.

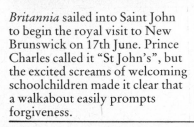

Brilliant colour abounded. Police reinforcements were called in to carry off the profusion of flowers given to the Princess, and the little girl and boy were charming in their period costume. She offered flowers to the Princess; he asked the Prince: "Where did you first meet your wife?"

There was plenty of noise too. On arrival, the deafening boom of the 21-gun salute was inescapable, the recoils screaming like Vimy Ridge. And the cheers and whistles from the 60,000 crowd were as incessant as their demands for attention, which slowed the royal progress to a virtual crawl.

Throughout it all it was good the see the Princess coping as easily and naturally with the demands, after only two years' experience, as her husband has after fourteen. Rothesay, where they visited the Collegiate School, offered a smartly-dressed and sweetly-singing girls' choir, and a ripping medley of Beatles' numbers by a local band. And, of course, a plethora of gifts, which included three coat-hangers – one for each Royal Highness in the family.

There was a State dinner that night at Saint John Convention Centre. Though marred by a comedy of errors of timing, and the indiscretions of a fulsome speech by New Brunswick's Premier, this otherwise magnificent and enjoyable occasion saw the Princess in shimmering turquoise, and the Prince in his usual good humour.

Royal weekends are often sacrosanct, but on Saturday 18th June the Prince and Princess flew to Charlo where a welcome, Red Indian style, awaited them. Buckskin-clad Micmac children danced a tribal greeting to the beat of a war-drum; chiefs in feathered head-dresses offered gifts of gloves and moccasins. A full deerskin outfit was handed over for Prince William. "He'll love it," promised the Princess.

A picnic lunch was eaten in Sugar Loaf Park, where crowds watched entertainments put on for the royal couple. No walkabout was scheduled, but it happened just the same.

One of New Brunswick's oldest
towns is St Andrews-by-sea – a
quaint fishing village by tradition
and latterly a seaside resort as
well. On Sunday 19th June its
damp mist hardly lifted as the
royal barge glided silently into its
harbour, but the local
population, some of whom had
been waiting seven hours, gave
the warmest of welcomes as the
Prince and Princess drove to All
Saints Church. As if taking its
cue, the weather cheered up –
relatively – to bright overcast.

The handsome, white, wooden church was surrounded, its grounds packed as rarely before in its 200-year history, long before the royal visitors arrived. For the vast majority without a seat inside the church, loudspeakers relayed the progress of the service, in which Prince Charles read the lesson.

It went without saying that a walkabout would follow, and the profusion of flags – Union Jacks and maple-leafs – made it a colourful one. On Fathers' Day, everyone wanted to know what Prince Charles (who complained of feeling old) had received from his wife. But he wasn't telling; nor was the Princess.

Whatever presents the Princess had given her husband, enough were offered today to sink the *Britannia*. Among those for Prince William was a small canoe which, according to his father, "he will be able to play with in his bath", and some fishing flies for Prince Charles. "If I'm not successful with them I can play with them in the bath as well," he joked. After the walkabout, the royal couple lunched at the Algonquin Hotel before leaving St Andrews as they had come – by barge.

The Prince and Princess sailed for Halifax, flying from there to Ottawa on 20th June. Parliament Hill was a blaze of colour and a buzz of excitement as 6,000 people watched the welcoming ceremonies in soaring temperatures.

The Princess of Wales wore a bright pink evening dress at the private reception given for her and Prince Charles by Premier Trudeau at Rideau Hall. It marked the end of their first day in Ottawa – one that had seen disappointingly low crowds, for which the intense humidity and comprehensive television coverage were blamed. But it was not without its surprises. The French-speaking community, usually conspicuous by their indifference to royalty, weighed in with as much fervour as anyone. They gave the Princess a new epithet – "sympathique".

Tuesday 21st June was Prince William's birthday. Before planting a tree at Rideau Hall and touring the Ottawa Police Headquarters, the Prince and Princess had been on the telephone to Kensington Palace, and heard "a few little squeaks" from their son.

Though plagued by questions about Prince William during a walkabout after the tree-planting ceremony, the royal couple seemed in good humour. But it was a comparatively quiet day, ending with a private barbecue at Kingsmere Farm (overleaf). Corn-cob and salmon was the royal choice.

"They're here!" trumpeted a local newspaper, against a photograph of the Prince and Princess disembarking from their plane at St John's, Newfoundland. The tour of the Maritime Provinces was resumed in typical conditions – St John's in fog, the Princess in pink, the crowds in ecstasies.

Sandwiched between the official welcomings and a Government House reception, the airport walkabout – the Canadians preferred to call it a talkabout – was the popular event of the afternoon. Ten-year-old Stephanie Sutton presented the bouquet, hands were stretched out, voices clamoured for recognition, the route from the airport was festooned with flags, balloons and banners – an apt welcome from the Empire's oldest territory.

That night the Prince and Princess rejoined *Britannia*, which had safely negotiated its way past an iceberg blocking St John's Harbour. The following day, 23rd June, nearly 7,000 youngsters and a guard of honour, uniformed 1812-style, welcomed them at the King George V Memorial Field, where Prince Charles opened the Youth Festival. The Princess seemed as embarrassed by having to join in some lusty sea-songs as by her husband's equally lusty revelations that he wanted more children! At the Memorial Stadium the royal couple were entertained again, and toured an exhibition put on by young people.

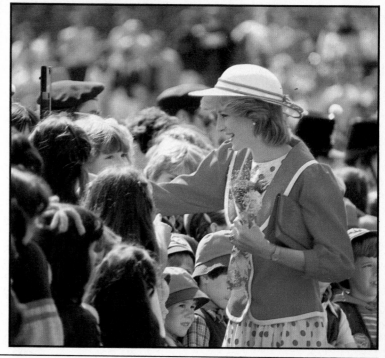

More formal duties took up the rest of the day. Prince Charles left the Princess on board *Britannia* when he returned to King George V Field to present new colours to the Royal Newfoundland Regiment, of which he has been Colonel-in-Chief for seven years. It was a nostalgic occasion, with strains of Auld Lang Syne and a parade of Royal Canadian Legion veterans. That evening the Princess was back in all her glory, attending an official banquet at the Newfoundland Hotel.

Prince Charles and his wife completely won over the Premier, Brian Peckford. At the banquet he was impressed by the Prince's knowledge of local affairs, and by the Princess' frank discussion of her long, difficult but successful apprenticeship.

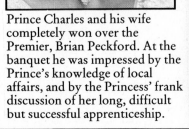

Newfoundland's capital was *en fête* on 24th June: it was St John's Day and its people were celebrating its 400th birthday. Predictably, on a tour noted for celebrating anniversaries, the Prince and Princess were at Canada Games Park to join in. Diana's bright green outfit perfectly matched the dazzle of the event, which the Prince opened. The usual complement of Canadian national flags and Union Jacks were swamped by the blue and white insignia commemorating this historic day. The release of thousands of balloons – Canada's favourite show of enthusiasm – ran into some initial trouble, but after a little prompting the sky was filled with bubbling colour.

The now familiar mists gathered in Cape Spear National Park that morning as the Prince and Princess went to see Newfoundland's oldest surviving lighthouse. Later, a massive floral arch hung with banners and flags welcomed them to City Hall for a buffet-luncheon.

Before rejoining *Britannia*, the royal couple launched into an impromptu walkabout on the dockside – an unexpected bonus for sightseers.

On their last day in Newfoundland the Prince and Princess visited Carbonear and Harbour Grace. At Carbonear they met all-comers, from very young children to veteran legionnaires, and seven-year-old Charmaine Dwyer's official posy was, as usual, not the only bouquet the Princess received. That afternoon the royal visitors sailed for Prince Edward Island.

Before leaving for Prince Edward Island the Prince and Princess took the unusual step of posing for photographs with members of *Britannia*'s crew who had served in the Falklands. It was the beginning of the only break the royal couple had – a day at sea before landing at Charlottetown on 27th June. Official welcomings and walkabouts started all over again.

A crowd of 5,000 hailed them rapturously on their arrival, and amid formal visits to Province House and the City Hall, and a tree-planting ceremony, the morning was full of pleasant incidents. Every child seemed to have flags to show the Princess, but one man upstaged them all: he leaned forward from the crowd, took the Princess' hand and kissed it.

The morning's three-hour schedule was separated, by a free afternoon, from the evening's event – a walkabout, programme of music and buffet-dinner in nearby Montague. Following her preference for informality, the Princess did not wear a hat.

And following the custom, Prince William's long list of official and unofficial gifts was supplemented by a rocking horse, presented by the Mayor of Montague.

The Prince and Princess' brief visit to Summerside began in true maritime fashion as the royal barge brought them to the Yacht Club's wharf. A local school band played during their walkabout —a grand sound compared with the lone bagpiper who greeted them at the Memorial Park later. That evening they watched track races at Charlottetown Driving Park (pages 126-7) and Prince Charles presented one of the prizes.

"Where better to spend your birthday than in Alberta," beamed Prince Charles, complimenting both his wife —two days short of her 22nd birthday— and Edmonton, where they had just arrived on 29th June. The 70,000 crowd gave them an almost hysterical welcome, and the Princess' striking red and white dress was much admired. The stiffish breeze which kept blowing her scalloped collar into her face proved a minor irritant.

Despite an alarm when the royal aircraft hit a stair-ramp on arrival at Edmonton, the Prince and Princess completed their walkabout in good spirits.

"Dress semi-formal, Klondike era," said the invitations for that evening's event, and Prince Charles and his lady were game enough to comply. He turned up in frock coat and side-creased trousers, waistcoat and cravat, spats and a silver-topped cane: she wore a whaleboned silk and lace dress with bustle and train, and long lace-up boots. There was a Gold-Rush-style music-hall entertainment in which the royal "couple of limeys" linked arms, sang and swayed to old-time numbers.

The main event of the evening was a barbecue in a marquee on the reconstructed site of Fort Edmonton. The Prince and Princess helped themselves to food, along with 850 guests.

This original event was a definite winner. "It may not be in the best royal tradition," said one Canadian, "but it beats the hell out of tree-planting." But the next day's ceremony to confer an Alberta University Doctorate of Laws on Prince Charles (overleaf) was almost as colourful.

Though indifferent weather during much of the tour may have been forgotten by then, rain fell again as Prince Charles and his wife attended a farewell banquet at Government House, Edmonton. But the Princess glowed in a gorgeous red dress and the Spencer tiara, and the Prince looked as proud of her as ever. A superb finale.

First English edition published by Colour Library Books Ltd.
© 1983 Illustrations and text: Colour Library International Ltd.
   99 Park Avenue, New York, N.Y. 10016, U.S.A.
This edition published by Greenwich House, a division of Arlington
House, Inc., distributed by Crown Publishers, Inc.
h g f e d c b a
Color separations by Reprocolor Llovet, Barcelona, Spain.
Printed and bound in Barcelona, Spain, by Cayfosa and Eurobinder.
ISBN 0-517-425440